WARNING!

DO NOT TRY THIS AT HOME!

WARNING!

WARNING!

WARNING!

CHALLENGES

PRANKS

OUTRAGEOUS

FILL-INS

WARNING!

DO NOT TRY THIS AT HOME!

CREATED BY

MICKEY & CHERYL GILL

FINE print
PUBLISHING

Fine Print Publishing Company
PO Box 916401
Longwood, Florida 32791-6401

Created in the USA & Printed in China
This book is printed on acid-free paper.

ISBN 9781-892951-98-4

2 3 5 7 9 10 8 6 4 1

fprint.net

DO NOT TRY THIS AT HOME . . .
unless you want to be the best prankster ever!

Deodorant that reeks, an impossible water trap, a vicious bug on the loose, and signs that keep everyone out. These are just some of the amazing pranks begging to be pulled!

And while plotting your next prank, you can challenge your bros, answer questions, and perform paper tricks.

Secre
Excellen

DO PRANK

Bros, brothers, and sisters (unless they're really little).

Bros who prank you. Cuz that's how it works!

DO NOT PRANK

Really young kids. That's not cool.

Older people like Grandpa and Grandma. It's not good for their health.

People with health problems. It's not good for their health either!

Strangers. That's just wrong!

ts to
Pranking

BE SMART

If someone's super scared of snakes, don't put a rubber snake in his closet!

BE SAFE

Never pull a prank that could hurt you or someone else.

STAY SNEAKY, NEVER GET CAUGHT, AND ALWAYS STAY ONE PRANK AHEAD OF YOUR BROS.

THE LEAKY PEN PROBLEM

1. Remove pen and ink spill from front of book.

PRANK ZONE

REMEMBER, WHEN YOU'RE NOT PULLING THIS PRANK, YOU CAN USE THE PEN. IT REALLY WORKS!

2. Set up the pen and ink spill on top of these items or areas and see what happens:

- ☐ Table cloth
- ☐ Driver's seat in car
- ☐ Stack of white towels
- ☐ Papers on desk
- ☐ Set of clean sheets
- ☐ Carpet or rug
- ☐ Stack of books
- ☐ Clothes
- ☐ Bedspread
- ☐ Couch

A WORD YOU CAN'T LIVE WITHOUT?

What or who do you wish could talk?

I have a lot to say.

YOU'RE ABOUT TO BE ZAPPED INTO SOMETHING NONHUMAN. WHAT DO YOU CHOOSE?

MOST TERRIFYING VILLAIN EVER?

What's Grossest?
- Long fingernails
- Bushy eyebrows
- Curly nose hairs?

Something ADULTS EAT that's just weird?

Would you fly to MARS if you could NEVER return to EARTH?
- YES!
- NO WAY!

Would you rather hide out in a
- Museum of Natural History (dinosaur bones, etc.)
- Secret laboratory
- Theme park?

1. Draw two equal-sized triangles on a big yellow sponge.

2. Cut out triangles.

3. Ice the top of each triangle with store-bought frosting.

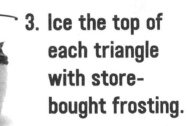

4. Stack one triangle on top of the other.

5. Frost down the sides.

Offer a slice to a bro!

ENTER THE
MAZE OF DOOM

HOW MANY TRIES DOES IT TAKE FOR YOU & YOUR BROS TO MAKE IT THRU IN 20 SECONDS OR LESS? WHO'S THE FASTEST?

KEEP SCORE!

SCOREBOARD

NAME	# OF ATTEMPTS	TIME

START HERE

FAST CASH

AND NOT-SO-LOOSE
CHANGE

1. Invite a bro over to your place.

2. Glue some coins down to a sidewalk or driveway close to your front door.

(Use white or clear glue. No superglue!)

PRANK ZONE

3. Tape some fishing line to
the back of a dollar bill
with transparent tape.
Place it next to coins.

4. Holding on to the other
end of the fishing line,
hide somewhere out of
sight and wait for your bro.

5. If he reaches for the dollar,
pull the fishing line. Then,
see if he goes for the coins.

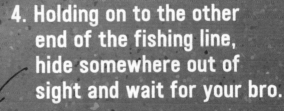

WEIRD questions

that won't make your brain hurt

What would you give up gaming for 1 month for?

WOULD YOU RATHER
- ☐ be the teacher's pet
- ☐ have a pet for a teacher?

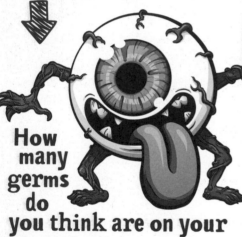

How many germs do you think are on your

TONGUE?

- ☐ None
- ☐ 10-20
- ☐ A BAGILLION!

SUPERHERO
you'd CHOW DOWN on chicken wings with?

[   ]

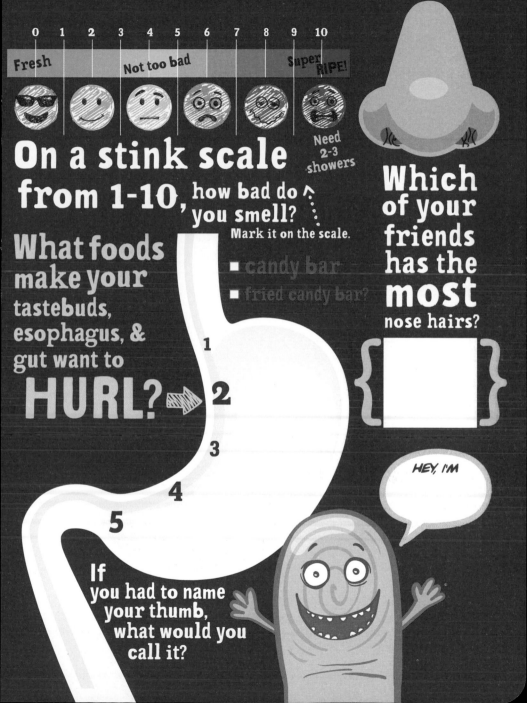

CRACKED TOILET SEAT!

PRANK ZONE

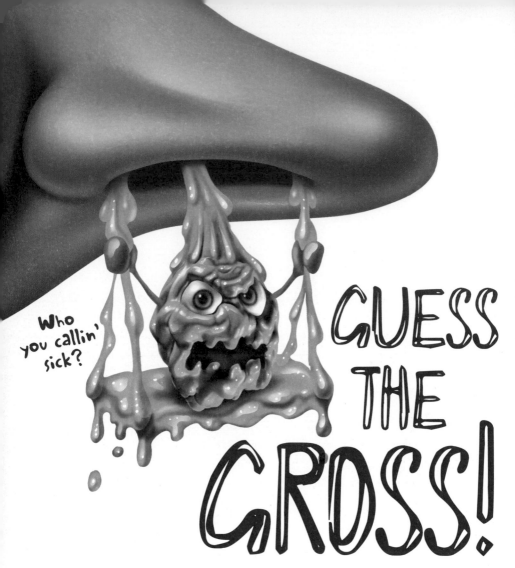

1. _____

2. _____

3. _____

4. _____

5. _____

6. _____

Answers at back of book

STINKY CHEESE ARMPITS!

WARNING:
USE AN EXTRA
STICK OF DEODORANT.
YOUR PRANKEE
NEEDS A GOOD
DEODORANT
BACKUP.

PRANK
ZONE

WALK THRU A PAGE IN THIS BOOK!

1. Cut this page out of the book, along the dotted line.

Follow instructions on the next page.

Fold page from right
to left along solid line.

Cut along dotted line.

2. Fold page from right to left along solid line.

3. Keeping paper folded, cut along the lines starting from the fold.

DO NOT CUT ALL THE WAY TO THE END!

4. Now, cut along the other set of lines.

5. Cut open each fold except the folds at each end.

Do not cut!
↓

Do not cut! ↓

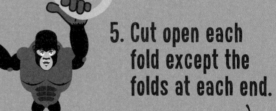

Open up the paper chain and **STEP** through it!

THE AMAZING
SPIDER

MANIA!

1. Cut out spiders and friends.

2. Attach transparent tape to back of bug.

3. Tape bug to the inside of light-colored drapes or lamps.

Wait for a scream!

PRANK ZONE

What's the CREEPIEST?

☐ RAT ☐ ROACH ☐ SPIDER

Pizza topping you are **NOT** interested in?

[   ]

BEST car ever?

[   ]

WORST car ever?

[   ]

Weirdest thing in your home?

DIRTIEST you've ever been?

Something invisible you wish you could see?

On a scale of 1-10, how are your dance moves?

1 2 3 4 5 6 7 8 9 10
Awful   Ok   Amazing!

Dessert you can totally walk away from?

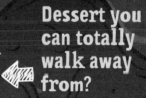

What are you deathly afraid of?

THE GREAT ESCAPE

1. Cut a small hole in a paper cup.

2. Turn it over on the kitchen counter.

3. Sprinkle paper cup scraps around hole.

4. Attach sticky note with warning message on it.

COCKROACH CHAOS!

1. Cut out a cockroach.

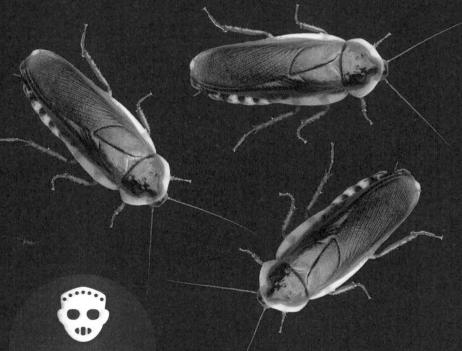

PRANK ZONE

2. Place it on the kitchen or bathroom counter.

3. Then hide a hard candy wrapper in your hand.

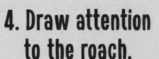

AHH! A ROACH! DON'T WORRY, I'LL GET IT!

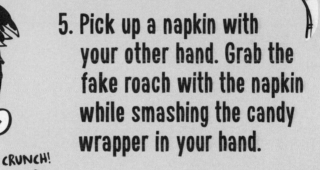

4. Draw attention to the roach.

5. Pick up a napkin with your other hand. Grab the fake roach with the napkin while smashing the candy wrapper in your hand.

CRUNCH! CRUNCH!

GOT IT!

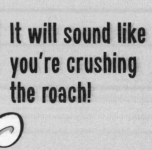

It will sound like you're crushing the roach!

NINJAS! KNIGHTS! ROBOTS! BROS!

How many ninjas can you & your friends spot in 20 seconds flat?
Then, find the others!

Keep score below				
NAME	Ninjas	Knights	Robots	Bros

Who got it right?
Correct total of groups at back of book

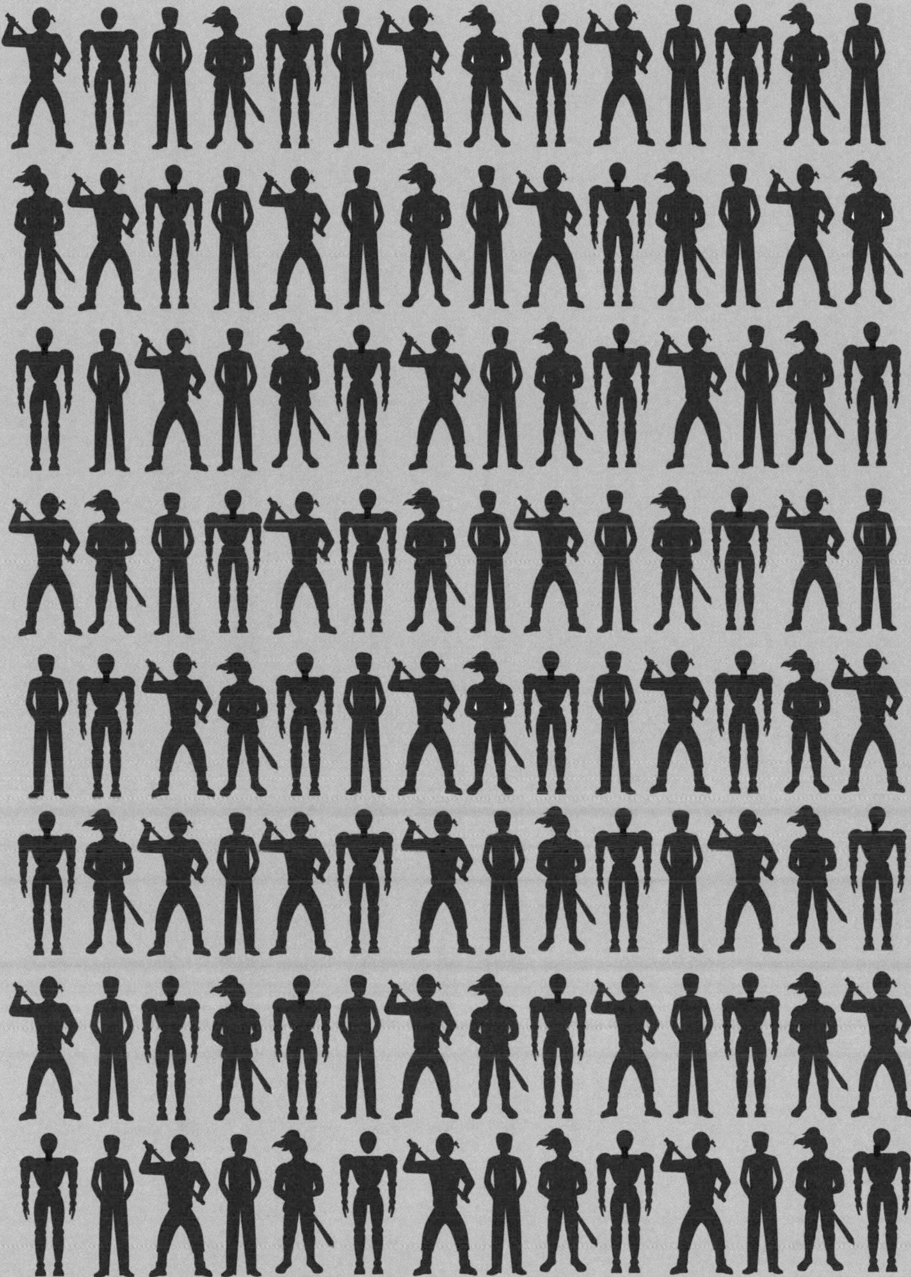

SHOCK

FRIENDS, FAMILY & TOTAL STRANGERS (WITH NO ELECTRICITY!)

1. Find a wall or area that does not have an electrical outlet.

2. Cut out an outlet. ----------->

3. Tape outlet to wall with transparent tape.

PRANK ZONE

WAIT TO SEE WHO TRIES TO USE IT!

FRIDGE FREAK OUT!

1. Write hilarious note on a brown bag.

2. Stuff bag with paper towels (to give it some weight).

3. Put bag in refrigerator.

If you could live **FOREVER** as a brain in a robot, would you do it?

☐ Yeah! ☐ No way, dude!

Besides FOOD & WATER, what could you not live without?

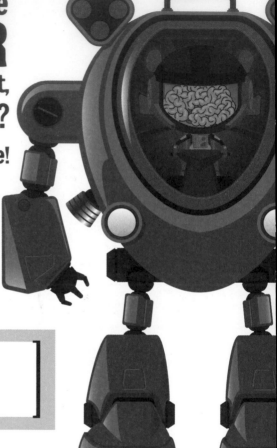

Which of these smells the worst? Your

☐ SNEAKERS ☐ BREATH ☐ BEDROOM

Would you rather eat

☐ CAT FOOD
☐ A ROTTEN APPLE
☐ PIZZA FROM THE GARBAGE?

What would be a better, more hilarious name for toilet paper?

[ ]

If you were an EMOJI, what would you be?

Animal body part that would be awesome to attach and detach when you wanted?

- ☐ GIANT BAT WINGS
- ☐ ALLIGATOR TAIL
- ☐ RHINO HORN

Would you rather have
- ☐ PINK HAIR
- ☐ RED TEETH?

If you owned a TANK, what would you name it?

[ ]

TOTALLY UNDERWATER

1. Drop a bro's key, Lego piece, or other small object into a clear glass.

PRANK ZONE

2. Fill glass with water, covering object.

3. **Place a piece of cardboard on top of glass. (Cardboard should completely cover opening.)**

4. **Holding cardboard against glass, flip glass onto kitchen counter or bathroom sink.**

5. **Quickly pull cardboard out from underneath glass.**

   Wait for bro to find it!

HA HA!

SQUIRT BLOCK!

CUT OFF ACCESS TO ALL CONDIMENTS!

1. Remove caps from squeeze bottle ketchup, mustard, mayo, or all three!

2. Wrap plastic wrap around bottle openings, place caps back on top of plastic wrap, and screw closed.

3. Cut off any plastic wrap that's showing.

ROACH II

Cut roaches out and place on top of a fruit bowl, on a refrigerator shelf, inside cupboards, or on a pillow.

PRANK ZONE

IVASION!

Tape to windows, doors, and mirrors.
Put a group of roaches on the bathroom floor.

MIND GAMES

DRIVE EVERYONE NUTS!

1. Switch clothes in drawers. Put socks in the t-shirt drawer, t-shirts in the sock drawer, and so on.

2. Move lamps, furniture, etc. just slightly over from usual position. Rearrange stuff on desk and dressers.

3. Change your clothes multiple times through-out the day. When someone notices, say, "What are you talking about?"

PRANK ZONE

AHH! WHAT'S GOING ON?!

PAPER PROPELLER
POWERED BY YOU!

LET'S DO THIS!

TRICK CENTRAL

START WITH A STORE RECEIPT LIKE THIS ONE.
IT'S ABOUT 3¼" WIDE X 6" LONG.

TIP

THE THINNER
THE PAPER,
THE BETTER.

WARNING:
DO NOT
USE YOUR
PARENTS'
RECEIPTS
WITHOUT
PERMISSION!

CANDY BASEMENT

YOUR ONE STOP SHOP
FOR ALL THINGS SWEET

TWIZZLERS	$4.99
SNOW CAPS	$2.50
SKITTLES	$3.99
GUMMY ROCKETS	$1.99
M&M'S	$3.59
RED HOTS	$1.99
	$19.05

DISCOUNT	$3.00
TOTAL	$16.05

THANK YOU!

TURN FOR INSTRUCTIONS ➡

1. FOLD RECEIPT OVER HERE.

2. THEN FOLD HERE AND HERE.

FOR ALL THINGS SWEET

TWIZZLERS	$4.99
SNOW CAPS	$2.50
SKITTLES	$3.99
GUMMY ROCKETS	$1.99
M&M'S	$3.59
RED HOTS	$1.99
	$19.05
DISCOUNT	$3.00

THANK YOU!

ALL THINGS SW

ZZLERS
W CAPS
TLES
MY ROCKETS
M'S
HOTS

THANK YOU!

CANDY BASEMENT

YOUR ONE STOP SHOP
FOR ALL THINGS SWEET

TWIZZLERS	$4.99
SNOW CAPS	$2.50
SKITTLES	$3.99
GUMMY ROCKETS	$1.99
M&M'S	$3.59
RED HOTS	$1.99
	$19.05
DISCOUNT	$3.00
TOTAL	$16.05

THANK YOU!

3. OPEN UP ALL FOUR FOLDS A BIT AND SLIGHTLY PINCH EACH CORNER.

(RECEIPT SHOULD LOOK KIND OF LIKE A LONG BOX WITHOUT A LID.)

TURN FOR MORE INSTRUCTIONS ➡

4. GRASP THE RECEIPT IN THE MIDDLE WITH YOUR THUMB AND MIDDLE FINGER. (MAKE SURE YOUR THUMB IS ON THE FRONT OF THE RECEIPT.)

FOLDS SHOULD FACE OUT. →

CANDY BASEMENT

YOUR ONE STOP SHOP
FOR ALL THINGS SWEET

TWIZZLERS $4.99
SNOW CAPS $2.50
SKITTLES $3.99
GUMMY ROCKETS $1.99
M&M'S $.59
RED HOTS

DISCOUNT $3.0
TOTAL $16.05

THANK YOU!

OOPS

OOPS   OOPS

I WISH I COULD

TRANSFORM

INTO

[   ]

WHENEVER I WANT.

I NEED A FOR

[   ]

AND I WANT TO
TURN UP
THE VOLUME ON

[   ]

Which bros would you call if you needed emergency backup?

_____

_____

_____

_____

IT WOULD BE WAY BETTER IF BOOGERS WERE

[ ]
color

I COULD TOTALLY **BEAT** ALL MY FRIENDS @

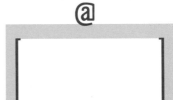

[ ]

A MOUNTAIN OF **MASHED POTATOES**

WOULD BE AMAZING WITH A MOUNTAIN OF

[ ]

1. Take apart a ball point pen that clicks.

2. Wad up a small piece of paper and toss into the empty barrel.

3. Put the pen back together.

TIP The pen should not be able to click. Try different sizes of paper wads until you find one that works.

SKULL AND CROSSBONE CHALLENGE

How fast can you move through these **3** levels and finally escape **SKULL CAVE?**

LEVEL 1 Move 1 bone to create another correct math problem.

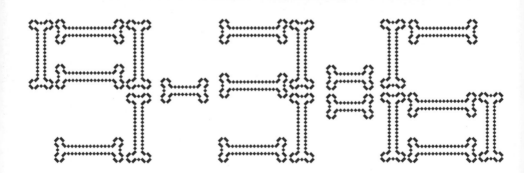

$$5 + 7 = 2$$

NEW MATH PROBLEM -

LEVEL 2 Solve this "skeletal remains" riddle.

You lead a group of 5 people into a cave full of bones. Two people get lost in the cave. One person stays with you. Two other people exit the cave. What color is the leader's hair?

START
HERE
⬇

LEVEL 3 Make your way through the maze and escape!

Answers at back of book

HIDDEN HORROR!

GET THEM WHEN THEY LEAST EXPECT IT!

1. Use transparent tape to hang a rubber snake from the top of a door inside a closet. Then shut the door.

2. Place plastic bugs (or paper roaches from this book) inside drawers in your home.

3. Put a big plastic lizard or dinosaur in the mailbox (after the mail is delivered and before someone gets it).

PRANK ZONE

TOILET MONSTER

1. Carefully pull this toilet monster poster out of book. See next page for more instructions.

2. Cut out toilet monster's hands.

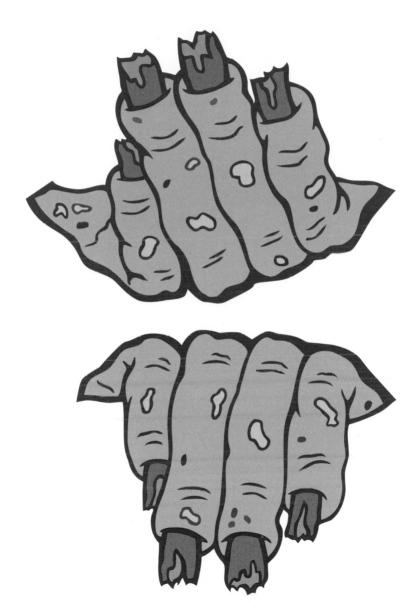

3. Lift toilet lid and seat.

4. Tape toilet monster face underneath seat with transparent tape. Put seat down.

5. Tape hands to top of seat with transparent tape. Then put lid down to hide monster.

Wait for scream!

BIGFOOT
OR
WEREWOLF?

Cut out signs and people figures.
Hang together on door like this.
Then flip over for a new image.

OR

Turn for more ⟶

Turn for more →

KEEP OFF THE GRASS

KOMODO DRAGON POOP EVERYWHERE

WARNING!
OPEN DOOR AT OWN RISK

ENTERING ANOTHER DIMENSION

GARAGE for SALE

WARNING!

FUNGUS EXPERIMENT IN PROGRESS

BEWARE
OF DOG
AND ITS FLEAS
AND TICKS

WARNING!

AREA
PATROLLED BY
RODEO
CLOWNS

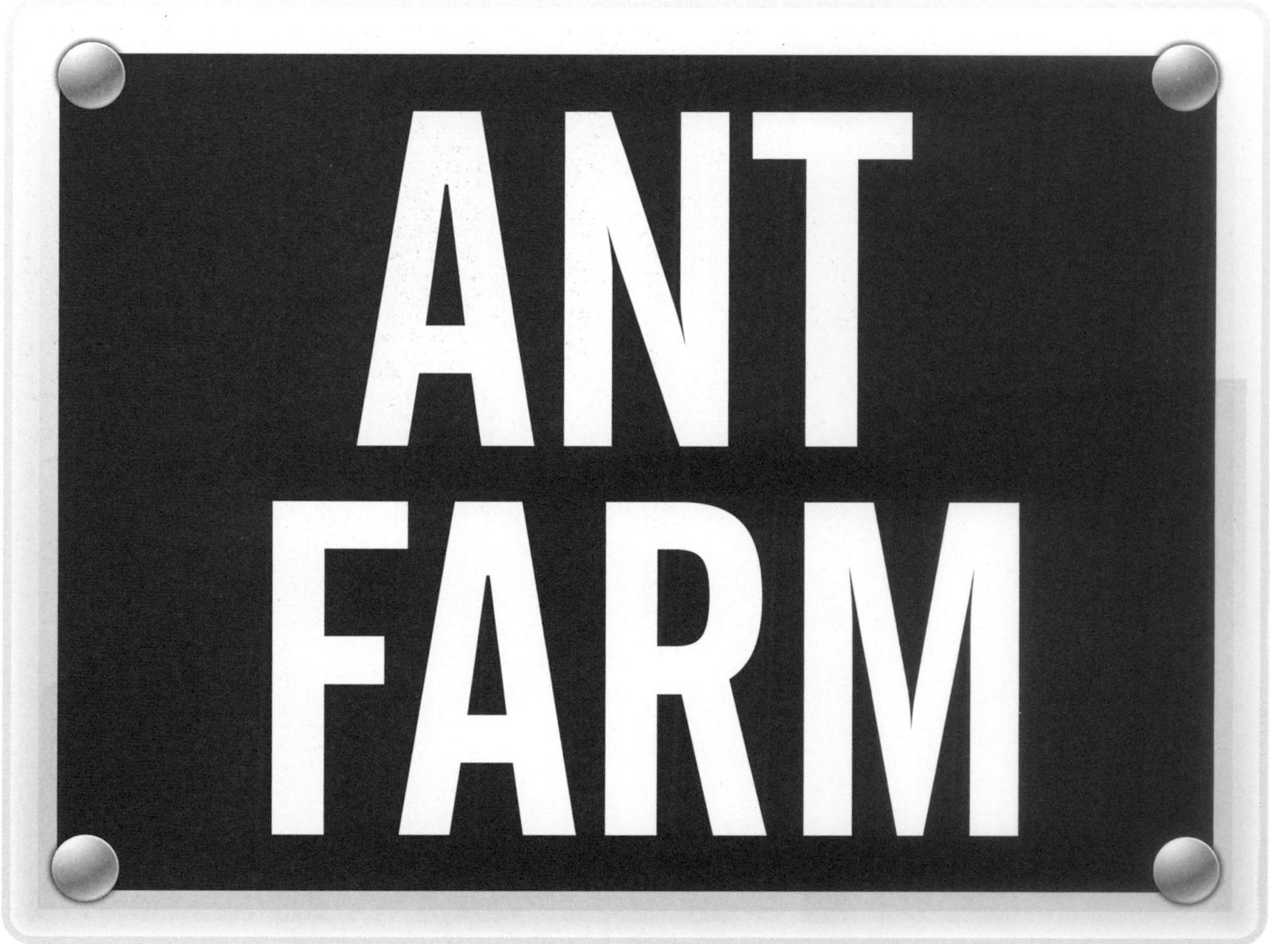
ANT
FARM

WARNING!

TICK

INFESTED AREA

DAYS WITHOUT A SHOWER!

MY RECORD IS ___ DAYS

LOOK TO THE LEFT

ENTER
VORTEX HERE

ANSWERS

GUESS THE GROSS!

1. Human brain
2. Maggots
3. Fish eggs
4. Mold
5. Mucus
6. Earwax

NINJAS! KNIGHTS! ROBOTS! BROS!

29 Ninjas
25 Knights
29 Robots
29 Bros

SKULL AND CROSSBONE CHALLENGE

LEVEL 1 –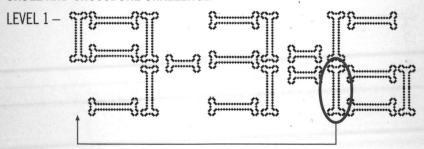

New math problem   8 - 3 = 5

LEVEL 2 – The leader's hair is your hair color because you are the leader.
（Read the first two words of the riddle.)